beyond my ken

beyond my ken

Joy McCall

A Stark Mountain Press Book

beyond my ken

Starkmtpress@gmail.com

No part of this book may be reproduced in any form
or by any means without permission in writing from
the publisher, except by a reviewer or scholar who
may quote brief passages in a review or article.

Front cover photo:
Castle Acre Benedictine Priory ruins,
Norfolk, England.
&
Back cover photo:
Dimwit on the holy roof and the moon

© Joy McCall 2023

Cover design by Larry Kimmel

ISBN: 979-8-3969543-4-2
Imprint: Independently published

beyond my ken*

*Old English *cennan* 'tell, make known'

I gather the things
beyond my ken
and scatter them
in the gorse and heather
on the wild moor

dedication

to Ryōkan Taigu

always my *anam cara**

*old Celtic word for my soul friend

poet's note –

Larry Kimmel suggested I make a book of my favourite tanka from my published books. Looking at all the many books, I thought it would be impossible, but it turned out to be very simple and quick.

The tanka I liked the most chose themselves. They were the ones that sang the songs of my own soul.

Joy

we have shared
a long road together
we have travelled miles
you are my friend
for this world and the next

Sandy Goldstein

the master says
I am magnificent
courageous
I creep back inside
the mousehole, trembling

Joy

beyond my ken

the moon
is hiding tonight
behind thin clouds
my wisdom is hiding
behind my fears

is my own pain
any different
than that borne
by the hunted hare,
the cornered fox?

I want to be
caught up in the wind
when I die
laughing, flying
sailing over the earth

in the circle
on the windy hill
a small box
and inside, a tied scroll
with the words 'there is no end'

my heart
sad at missing him
glad with love
the fish as always
swims upstream and down

I wonder
about friendship
and I find
the old English 'sciepe' –
the shape of a thing

aphasia
all those lost words
I could not find
coming back, marching
in five straggly lines

small brown bird
picking at moss seeds
in the rain –
oh why am I not
more like you?

I would be
a sweeper of church floors
working slow
in shadows and silence
alone with gods and ghosts

the poet said
'you must write forever'
and a vision comes
of a pale skeletal hand
in the grave, holding a pen

a tiny bone
caught in brambles
on the common path
I take it to the churchyard
and bury it there

the mala string
back on its iron hook
by the fire
swings gently, sending
my last silent prayers

reading
Taigu Ryōkan
as dusk falls
here, too the thief
left behind the waning moon

I rang the bells
again and again tonight
for my friend
they will not disturb his sleep
deep underground

he will show up
in some corner
of my heaven
a wild dandelion
in a narrow field of grass

sweetgrass braids
western red cedar bark
juniper leaves
white sage, forest pine
and wild, wild thyme

now and then
the old grief
wells up
deep in my soul
'I want to walk'

still not ready
for these grinding bones
to be grey ash
I find an old hand
to pull me from the fire

am I
a mouse dreaming
I'm a woman
or a woman
dreaming I'm a mouse?

(after Zhuangzi)

my tattoos –
flying fish, diving birds
swimming snakes
as if I knew
walking would be lost

pondering
on the wabi-sabi
of poetry
the fading beauty
the words still singing

doubting God
as Thomas did
so long ago
and yet … the field mice
the beetles, the sky

when we lose hope
in the great races
of humanity
let us look down
at the ants in the grass

my brief poems
are like gnats
blown
on the wind –
they come, they go

solitary
in his prison cell
he writes to me
'I am trapped' and he knows
paralysed, I understand

my daughters have come
not only from my body
but from some far distant soul
they shine like stars
in the darkest of nights

writing
in a small notebook
words I love
page after page –
windswept … truth … moss …

cocoa
witch hazel
wild thyme
I'm not a woman
whose scent is roses

blue jay feather
river otter bone
side by side
we are bones
we are flight

the candle
is burning low
in the pan
the copper grows warm
a song forms in the smoke

still there is
holiness
in the dark –
where else
does the light come from?

far away music
carried on the evening breeze
ripples on the pond
a glimpse of a hem of silk
at the closing of the door

my creed?
never judge
meet each need
with honest love
find joy, harm none

in the old warehouse
his battered harmonica
sits on the bench
with empty bourbon bottles
he plays, drunk, Kentucky blues

dreams gather and settle
inside these wooden boxes
oak, pine, fir
red cedar, dark walnut
fragments, traces of the trees

the high altar
is not accessible
for the likes of me –
cripples and sinners sit
outside the circle

by the ancient yew
the woodcarver stands
closing his eyes, he steps through
and on the other side
anything is possible

long-legged
among the butterflies
he stands
shoulder blades morphing
into frail blue wings

(for Brian Zimmer)

I wish I had skin
the colour of sand, the coat
of a brown-eyed doe
or my pale bones covered
with a hen's feathers

we dance
on the thin edge
of dark woods
take my hand lest I fall
into the thorny briars

the dark man walks
through all my days and nights
casting a long shadow
the pale woman watches him
from her hiding place, yearning

he says
holy simplicity
is the only way
I follow his shadow
across the flagstones

I am a tree
a patch of moss
some rain
the grey smoke rising
from a low campfire

blow out the candle
watch the thin smoke rising
like a small spirit
in the still twilight room –
ancestors are drawing near

my heart has broken
many times, and growing old
I try to mend it
with something that shines
the gold of kintsugi

things of the edges
that hide in dark shadows
things sensed, not seen
the feeling someone is near
that slight turning in the heart

how come
I make friends with crooks
priests and witches?
I love the dark, the light
and the shadows in between

I learn from Osho
and from the old monk
to trust life –
the wind, the land
the air, the rain

burning
a small chunk
of cedar wood
I hear a voice – 'trust,
listen to the wind'

I say a poem
must be simple enough
for a child to pick up
and pass, in small hands
to the old, the lost, the dying

does the dove
watching the dusk owl
long to hoot?
why can I not be content
with my own song?

I will go and hold out
my broken hands
and heart
to the gods of rain
and wind, on the hill

my deer spirit
is dead, lying broken
beside the road
the mouse runs quick away
along the greening verge

once I was doe
and silver minnow
and racing hare
now in wood and field
I'm a small brown mouse

reclaiming
the word 'cripple'
for myself
I feel strangely at home
in my flesh and bones

touching wood
crossing my fingers
these hard times –
the manger, the cross
the coffin, the pyre

the dear voices
of the dead are everywhere
listen now –
across the strait the monks
are chanting vespers

so I be rowan
you be ash, bending
in the northern winds
life and bravery be ours
green plains, ruined towers

I lift the coracle bell
that hangs by the holy fire
it warms my hands
and rings, and takes me
to the mossy Shinto shrine

all these words
scrambling about in my head
when I sleep –
I wish they would form
an orderly line

the nave has fallen
the tower still stands
the bell rings
on cold windy nights
thin holy ghosts are praying

a quiet spell
herbs burning on the hearth –
rosemary
and hawthorn berry
a prayer for our suffering earth

sweetgrass
burning in the bowl
grey smoke
rising slow
an old prayer

the medics
are baffled by the fire
in my bones
I go looking
for a witch doctor

among the trees
the soft mosses, the shrubs
the new spring leaves
I am the same small mouse
happy in harusaki

(springtime)

reading Ray Bradbury –
Swedish mother, English father
descended
from a hanged witch
no wonder I relate!

in the quietness
of woods, fields and ruins
I hear
the whispering of holy truth –
God's voice in leaf and stone

that word
I love so much – holy
Old English *hālig*, Germanic,
from Dutch and German *heilig* ...
I'm a speck in the Whole

those shelters and bulwarks
we make to keep our souls
and spirits safe
can be so lovely that they shine
like stained glass, like old hymns

the night winds
are blowing the bells that hang
from the garden trees ...
I'm back in the northern circle
hearing sheep bells on the far hills

Yi tells me
I must keep my dark
lest my dual nature catch fire –
that will be easy for this fish
who so loves the shadows

reality
has crashed and split
the dream in two
but look at the gold
deep in the chasm

I wonder
if I scattered my poems
on the ground
would they rot like leaves
and make a home for beetles?

please
pardon the monster
howling at the door
he too is sad
and needs a friend

the priest is chanting
among the gravestones
by the ruined church
and in the old yew tree
a blackbird starts to sing

my heart
is filled with sadness
my head with thoughts
how I long for
a simple soul

a quiet inner voice says
there are possibilities
of which you know
nothing at all; let her go –
the wind is calling

I cry out
where are you?
her voice says
'I am light
watch me shine'

(Wendy)

we talk of wind
and snow and pine cones
and monks
songs and silence
the moon, the seashore

the horse and the doe
hide in the shadows
the bright eyes
of the black raven
watch over them

(Wendy, Joy, Kate)

past midnight
I should sleep
but oh ...
the wind, the owls
the little train

I would
want a heart,
not of gold
but of rain, wind
and feathers

the full snow moon
shines on the old asylum
and in its light
the lunatics still sing
dancing down the long hall

two decades
since last my foot
touched the earth
yet I feel the soil,
the stones, the bones

I long
for a hermitage
in far mountains
with the cry of the deer
and the wind in the pines

in the old church
pale light through stained glass
quiet still air
we light candles
for our loved ones

I grow older
on the surface
and yet
within me, a child sings
a girl dances

the clock creeps
slowly to midnight
the witching hour
I sing softly to myself
'now the green blade rises'

I look at the old scroll
on my wall – the crane
at island's end
and I wonder, is there a bird
waiting to take my soul to heaven?

the ruined shrine
home to mosses
and wild deer
still calls my name
begging me to come

'the cradle
for the body is nature'
said Susumo ...
I settle to sleep in
hawkweed and feathers

where do we turn
when we need help?
to the deep pools
of love that hide
in all the shadows

Afterword

There is an immensity of reality that is beyond our knowing, yet what shines through in Joy McCall's latest collection is the many connections, relationships and shared circumstances that join us to each other, to all lives and to all those who have passed and gone before us. Our bond to Mother Earth and the spirits of our ancestors inhabit the tanka of 'beyond my ken' as does an empathic kinship with the many creatures we share this planet with.

Joy McCall has been reading, writing, breathing, thinking, talking in tanka her whole adult life. A born poet, her interest in poetry began in childhood and she has become the most prolific tanka poet in English alongside her dear friend in tanka, Sanford Goldstein.

'beyond my ken', represents her selection of her tanka that represent the best most personal range of her 'voice' and being. Readers will discover what is most precious and everlasting from her transcendent and miraculous life. Joy has written thousands of tanka and from those thousands is this, a well-chosen set of ninety-four tanka.

Joy has a deep compassion for her creaturely neighbors and has long felt a closeness and abiding connection, especially, to mice, deer

and all types of birds. The significance of the
creatures that inform her tanka provide the
presence of owls, doves, gnats, butterflies, ants,
beetles, fish, snakes and horses to name a few.

my tattoos
flying fish, diving birds
swimming snakes …
as if I knew
walking would be lost

Within this collection you will also meet her
daughters, monks, priests, Ryokan, Osho, Ray
Bradbury, ghosts, gods, crooks, witches, lunatics,
Susumo, and children.

You will visit moors, churches, mouseholes,
windy hills, streams, churchyards, fields, forests,
prisons, ponds, warehouses, campfires, ruins,
towers, shrines, mountains and hermitages.

All along this tanka path, Joy's path, there is love,
unending love and emotional connections,
talismans, pains, burdens, wishes, dreams, fears,
circles, small boxes, smoke, shadows, moons,
grief and songs. Her tanka are graced in humility
and the kindred confessions of a poet in awe and
love with life, even a life in which she has dealt
with long term physical limitations, due to a
motorcycle accident twenty years ago, that left
her unable to walk.

now and then
the familiar grief
wells up
deep in my soul
'I want to walk'

There is a thread that runs throughout 'beyond my ken' that is the heart and soul of Joy McCall whispering, communing and expressing the very breadth of her experiences and inspirations. In tanka turns she holds a candle out in the dark for us to see and feel both the intimacy of her life and through the open window into our own lives.

When you enter into Joy's tanka time you can and will be drawn into timeless places within where you begin to recognize our collective place among all creatures who are our sacred relations.

With brilliant vision and revelations, the tanka in 'beyond my ken' invite readers to look deep within themselves and recognize just how much we can find within ourselves. A significant part of our life is the search for meaning and to decipher the mysteries and wonders of all that is *beyond our ken.*

This collection serves as the reconciliations and admissions from one lovely and devoted poet who has divined her way in this life and world, poem by poem.

It is a tribute to Joy, having written as many tanka as she has, that she was able to pick out these ninety-four. A deep bow to her and to each reader who takes the time to know Joy through her tanka and beautifully learn more about themselves by doing so. This collection provides us with a poetic key to what is *beyond our ken.*

pondering
on the wabi-sabi
of poetry
the fading beauty
the words still singing

in the circle
on the windy hill
a small box
and inside, a tied scroll
with the words 'there is no end'

*

As Albert Einstein beautifully articulated:

"A human being is a part of the whole called by us universe, a part limited in time and space. He experiences himself, his thoughts and feeling as something separated from the rest, a kind of optical delusion of his consciousness. This delusion is a kind of prison for us, restricting us to our personal desires and to affection for a few persons nearest to us. Our task must be to free ourselves from this prison by widening our circle of compassion to embrace all living creatures and the whole of nature in its beauty."

Tom Clausen
Ithaca, New York
poet, photographer and witness ...

June 2023

<>

"The dark feelings for one's self and one's loved ones at the far edge of this life on earth are always in the wings."

*

dusk
and the day lily all but done

Larry Kimmel

<>

Acknowledgments

These poems all come from published books. I owe a great debt of gratitude to Keibooks, Skylark books, Mousehold Press, hedgerow books, Nick at Gowise Print, and my good friend Larry Kimmel at Stark Mountain Press, who have all helped my words travel out into the wide tanka world.

Joy

About the Author

Joy was born in Norwich towards the end of WW2. She lived in several English towns in her youth as her father was a roving vicar.

Joy moved to Amherst, Massachusetts in 1966 when she married Brian who was at Amherst College, and from there on to Toronto, Canada where she later lived as a single mum with her two daughters. They moved back to Norwich a couple of decades later, where Joy met and married Andy, 30 years ago.

Her older daughter Kate lives in Canada and very sadly Joy's younger daughter Wendy has recently lost her brave battle with multiple sclerosis. Joy's younger brother David Street died this winter in Norwich after fighting his own courageous battle with cancer. Joy herself is a paraplegic amputee after an accident in 2002.

Her strength comes from her loved ones and from nature and from poetry. Her favourite old poets are Ryôkan and Frances Cornford.

Joy is a Pisces.

<>

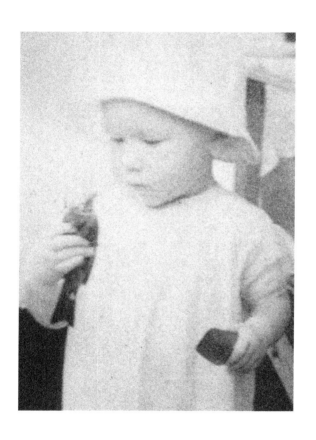

Joy aged 2, communing with a dead bird

Other books by Joy McCall
(available on Amazon)

the well-worn path (out of print)
heartsongs (out of print)
the Animus Thief with Pete Bromage
sun songs with Gwen Burch
pine winds, autumn rain with Orrin PréJean
(Matsukaze)
mandalas – pictures
singing into darkness with Liam
    Wilkinson
on the cusp
on the cusp encore
see how they run
circling smoke, scattered bones
rising mist, fieldstones
this is my song - tanka prose
hedgerows - sequences
fieldgates – sequences
things of the edges
sweetgrass and thyme
touching the now with Don Wentworth
hagstones with Claire Everett
is it the wind that howls? with Liam
    Wilkinson
beetles and stars with Jenny Ward Angyal
    and Claire Everett
the beauty of rust with Bill Albert
    and Paul Levy
stillness lies deep with Tim Lenton
Norfolk ways with Tim Lenton

nogusa
kotoba
ochiba
side by side with Larry Kimmel
the woodpile dwindling with Gwen Burch
borderlands
ripples
circling
the chill of time
twilight
daybreak
a worn chest with Tom Clausen
in the mountain's shadow with Issa
   and Don Wentworth
into the winter wood with Jonathan Day
calling forth the light with Denis Garrison
the last mile on the tanka road
   with Sanford Goldstein

Printed in Great Britain
by Amazon